BE SEATED

God Will Make Your Enemies Your Footstool

PASTOR DR. CLAUDINE BENJAMIN

For more information or to book an event, contact:
inspiredtowinsouls@gmail.com

Published by:

Editor: Cleveland O. McLeish (Author C. Orville McLeish)

ISBN: 978-1-965635-71-1 (paperback)

About the Author

Pastor Claudine Benjamin is a servant of God with a burning passion to see lives transformed by the power of the gospel. She has devoted her life to proclaiming the uncompromising Word of God, equipping believers to walk in their divine authority, and calling the church back to its original mandate—to win the lost at any cost.

A voice of boldness and compassion, Pastor Benjamin ministers with prophetic clarity, practical wisdom, and a deep love for the people of God. Her writings reflect her heartbeat for revival, discipleship, and spiritual empowerment. She firmly believes that every believer is called to live seated in victory with Christ, no longer beneath the weight of opposition, but above it, reigning in life through Him.

Through her books, messages, and ministry, Pastor Benjamin speaks to the broken, the weary, and the warrior, reminding them that God turns every trial into triumph, every storm into strength, and every enemy into a footstool. Her unique ability to blend scripture, personal insight, and spiritual urgency has touched countless lives and continues to inspire a new generation of kingdom laborers.

When she is not writing or preaching, Pastor Benjamin is devoted to mentoring, intercessory prayer, and strengthening the body of Christ to remain steadfast in faith. She is known for her relentless pursuit of God's presence, her unwavering belief in the power of prayer and fasting, and her conviction that revival begins with one surrendered life.

Her prayer is that every reader of her works will rise into the fullness of their calling, embrace their heavenly position, and live in the unstoppable victory promised through Christ Jesus.

Dedication

This book is lovingly dedicated to the King of kings and Lord of lords, Jesus Christ, who is seated at the right hand of the Father, reigning in eternal glory. To Him belongs all power, authority, and dominion, both now and forevermore.

I also dedicate these pages to every believer who has ever felt pressed down by the weight of enemies, circumstances, or spiritual battles. May you find through these words the assurance that your life is hidden in Christ, that your position is one of victory, and that your enemies are already destined to become your footstool.

Finally, I dedicate this work to the next generation of warriors, intercessors, and soul winners who will carry the mantle of bold faith. May this book remind you that your place is not beneath the enemy's feet but above, seated with Christ in heavenly places.

Acknowledgment

With a heart full of gratitude, I pause to give thanks:

- To Almighty God for the revelation, strength, and grace to complete this work. Without His Spirit's leading, these words would be lifeless, but with His breath, they carry fire, authority, and truth.

- To my family and loved ones, thank you for your prayers, encouragement, and support as I poured out my heart into these pages. You are my earthly footstools of strength, steadying me when the weight was heavy.

- To the body of Christ, especially faithful intercessors, pastors, and leaders who continue to preach, teach, and contend for the faith once delivered to the saints. Your labor is not in vain. May this book strengthen your hands for the battle and your hearts for the harvest.

- To every reader, thank you for opening these pages and allowing the message of Hebrews 1:13 to speak into your spirit. My prayer is that you will not only read these words but rise up in your God-given authority, resting in Christ while advancing His kingdom with boldness.

Above all, to God alone be the glory. May every testimony, breakthrough, and transformation that results from this book return to Him as a sweet offering of praise.

Table of Contents

Part IV

Living in Triumph

Part V

Eternal Victory

Introduction

"But to which of the angels said he at any time, Sit on my right hand, until I make thine enemies thy footstool?" — Hebrews 1:13 (KJV)

There is a command that echoes from eternity's throne room—a divine invitation to rest, a summons to authority, and a promise of victory: **"Sit at my right hand, until I make your enemies your footstool."**

This single verse captures the heart of the believer's position in Christ. It is not a call to strive endlessly, to battle in human strength, or to live in constant fear of defeat. Instead, it is a call to take our rightful place—seated with Christ in heavenly places—while God Himself ensures that every enemy is subdued beneath His feet.

Too many believers live their lives fighting battles that Christ has already won. They wrestle with fear, doubt, rejection, opposition, and spiritual warfare, forgetting that the cross has already secured victory. The throne is not empty. Christ is not standing in worry or pacing in anxiety. He is seated, enthroned in triumph. And if He is seated, then so are we.

This book, **Be Seated: God Will Make Your Enemies Your Footstool**, is a journey into that divine posture. It will explore what it means to live from the throne and not from fear, to reign in Christ's authority rather than strive in self-effort, and to see every

11

enemy—whether sin, Satan, fear, rejection, or even death itself—placed under the feet of the King.

You will discover through scripture, revelation, and application that:

- **Your position is secure** — seated with Christ, not beneath the enemy's power.

- **Your enemies are temporary** — destined to become stepping stones and testimonies.

- **Your authority is real** — given by the King of kings for victorious living.

- **Your hope is eternal** — anchored in the coming day when every enemy, including death, will be destroyed forever.

This is not a book of empty encouragement but of prophetic truth. It is a call to the weary believer to rest, to the fearful heart to rise in boldness, and to the church to walk in the authority of her seated King.

As you read each chapter, my prayer is that you will sense chains falling, fears breaking, and confidence rising. May you walk away not only with knowledge but with transformation—seated in Christ, resting in His victory, and walking in His authority.

The throne is occupied. The footstool is promised. The victory is certain.

Beloved, it is time to be seated.

Part I

The Power of the Promise

Chapter One

The King's Command: Sit at My Right Hand

"But to which of the angels said He at any time, Sit on my right hand, until I make thine enemies thy footstool?" — Hebrews 1:13 (KJV)

THE INVITATION TO SIT

The command "Sit at My right hand" is more than a royal decree; it is a divine invitation. In ancient kingdoms, sitting at the king's right hand was the highest position of honor, authority, and partnership. This verse, quoted from **Psalm 110:1**, is the Father's declaration to His Son, Jesus Christ, after the work of redemption was accomplished. Unlike angels who minister as servants, Christ was told to sit. He was not called to strive, struggle, or fight for His throne; He was commanded to rest, because the victory had already been secured.

This same invitation extends to every believer. Through Christ's finished work, we too are called to live from a seated position, not frantic activity, but restful authority. Ephesians 2:6 confirms this truth: **"And hath raised us up together, and made us sit together in heavenly places in Christ Jesus." (KJV).** To sit is to trust. To sit is to rest in confidence that God Himself is bringing every enemy into subjection.

REST AFTER VICTORY, NOT BEFORE THE BATTLE

When God said to Christ, "Sit at My right hand," the cross had already been endured, the blood had already been shed, and the resurrection had already secured eternal triumph. Sitting was not the beginning of His fight, but the posture after victory.

For us, this becomes a lesson in perspective. Too often, we try to sit before the battle, desiring peace without endurance, or we refuse to sit after the battle, continuing to strive when God has already given the victory. The command is not an option but a divine order: "Sit." The believer's strength does not come from restless activity, but from resting in the certainty that God is working.

Isaiah 30:15 declares, **"In returning and rest shall ye be saved; in quietness and in confidence shall be your strength." (KJV).** Sitting, then, is not weakness—it is the strongest position a believer can hold.

THE AUTHORITY OF THE RIGHT HAND

The right hand of God symbolizes power and authority. To be seated at the Father's right hand is to share in His reign, His dominion, and His victory. Psalm 98:1 proclaims, **"O sing unto the Lord a new song; for he hath done marvellous things: his right hand, and his holy arm, hath gotten him the victory." (KJV).**

Christ did not seize this authority; it was bestowed upon Him. Likewise, we cannot earn or manufacture spiritual authority—it is given to us by virtue of our union with Christ. Our position at the right hand of God is not a future promise but a present reality. The enemy may still rage, but he is already a defeated foe.

THE WAITING OF FAITH

The Father's promise was clear: **"Until I make your enemies your footstool."** Notice that God Himself takes responsibility for this act. The Son is not commanded to fight His enemies but to wait in trust. The enemies are real, the opposition is fierce, but the outcome is guaranteed.

This is the tension of faith: learning to sit while God works. Many believers struggle with this waiting period, feeling the urge to rise and fight in their own strength. Yet the call is clear: wait, trust, and remain seated. Waiting is not inactivity; it is active trust. It is the faith-filled refusal to abandon the throne for the battlefield when the King has already promised victory.

APPLICATION FOR THE BELIEVER

1. **Rest in Christ's Finished Work** – Stop striving for what Christ has already accomplished. You are seated in heavenly places, and victory is already assured.

2. **Trust God's Timing** – Do not be anxious if enemies still seem present. The process of making them a footstool is God's work, not yours.

3. **Maintain the Posture of Faith** – Sitting requires humility and confidence. Stand in authority through prayer, but sit in trust through rest.

4. **Live from the Throne, Not the Battlefield** – See your life through the lens of victory, not constant warfare. Your posture changes your perspective.

REFLECTION

1. Where in your life are you still standing in your own strength when God has already told you to sit?

2. Are there battles you are fighting in the flesh that God has already promised to win in the spirit?

PRAYER

Father, thank You for inviting me to sit with Christ at Your right hand. Teach me to rest in Your authority and not to strive in my own strength. Help me to trust Your timing as You bring every enemy under my feet. May I live daily from a place of victory, peace, and confidence, knowing that You are faithful to Your promise. In Jesus' name. Amen.

Chapter Two

The Heavenly Throne and the Earthly Footstool

"Thus saith the Lord, The heaven is my throne, and the earth is my footstool: where is the house that ye build unto me? and where is the place of my rest?" — Isaiah 66:1 (KJV)

THE THRONE ABOVE ALL

Heaven is the dwelling place of God's glory, the seat of His authority, and the throne of His eternal rule. The prophet Isaiah records the Lord's words: **"The heaven is my throne."** Thrones represent sovereignty and dominion. For God to declare heaven as His throne means that His rulership extends over all creation. Nothing escapes His oversight. Nothing stands beyond His reach.

The throne is a picture of unshakable stability. While earthly thrones and governments shift, collapse, and are replaced, God's throne remains forever. Psalm 45:6 declares, **"Thy throne, O God, is for ever and ever: the sceptre of thy kingdom is a right sceptre." (KJV).** Believers draw confidence from this eternal throne, knowing that the One who reigns is righteous, just, and faithful.

THE EARTH AS HIS FOOTSTOOL

Equally striking is the image of the earth as God's footstool. In ancient culture, a footstool symbolized complete subjugation. To place one's feet upon something was to demonstrate dominion over it. By calling the earth His footstool, God reveals that all of creation, all kingdoms, and all enemies are under His feet.

The writer of Hebrews echoes this imagery when speaking of Christ: **"Until I make thine enemies thy footstool" (Hebrews 1:13 - KJV).** The throne represents God's position of authority, but the footstool demonstrates His victory. In other words, what seems chaotic on earth is already subject to the reign of heaven.

This truth changes our perspective. What we see as battles, trials, and strongholds, God sees as material for His footstool. Our enemies are not equal rivals to God; they are stepping stones beneath His feet.

BIBLICAL ILLUSTRATIONS OF THRONE AND FOOTSTOOL

1. **Solomon's Throne** (see 2 Chronicles 9:17–18): The great throne of Solomon was elevated with a footstool of gold attached to it, symbolizing the king's complete dominion. This earthly picture foreshadows the heavenly reality of Christ's eternal throne.

2. **Joshua's Conquest** (see Joshua 10:24): When five kings opposed Israel, Joshua called his captains to place their feet on the necks of the defeated kings. This act symbolized

complete subjugation—a powerful preview of Christ making every enemy His footstool.

3. **Christ's Resurrection** (see Acts 2:34–35): Peter quotes Psalm 110:1, declaring that God has exalted Jesus to His right hand and promised to make His enemies His footstool. The resurrection sealed this victory, proving that heaven rules earth.

APPLICATION POINTS

1. **Heaven Rules Earth** – No matter what chaos surrounds me, heaven's throne governs earth's affairs. I must see situations through God's perspective.

2. **My Enemies Are Already Under His Feet** – The devil may roar, but he is already defeated. Trials may arise, but they are being transformed into God's footstool.

3. **My Worship Connects Heaven and Earth** – When I worship, I acknowledge God's throne and submit earthly matters beneath His authority. Worship shifts my vision from the footstool to the throne.

REFLECTION

• Do you focus more on the chaos of the earth or the stability of heaven's throne?

• In what areas of your life do you need to remind yourself that God already has His feet on the matter?

- How can you worship in a way that brings your earthly struggles under God's heavenly authority?

PRAYER

Lord, I honor You as the King whose throne is in heaven and whose feet rest upon the earth. Teach me to live with confidence in Your authority and not in fear of earthly troubles. Help me to see every trial as part of the footstool You are building under Your feet. May my life of worship bring glory to Your throne and remind me daily that heaven rules over earth. In Jesus' name. Amen.

Chapter Three

Enemies Under His Feet: A Prophetic Fulfillment

"The Lord said unto my Lord, Sit thou at my right hand, until I make thine enemies thy footstool." — Psalm 110:1 (KJV)

THE PROPHETIC PROMISE

Psalm 110:1 is one of the most quoted Old Testament verses in the New Testament. Written by David under the inspiration of the Spirit, it foretold the exaltation of Christ to the Father's right hand and the eventual subjugation of His enemies. For centuries, Israel recited this psalm, not fully grasping that it pointed directly to the Messiah.

When Jesus rose from the grave and ascended into heaven, this prophecy came alive. God Himself placed Christ at His right hand, the highest seat of authority, and began the process of bringing every enemy into subjection. Hebrews 1:13 confirms this fulfillment, distinguishing Christ's exaltation from angelic service.

This is not just prophecy fulfilled in Christ's life—it is prophecy that continues to unfold in the believer's life. Every enemy of God's people is destined to bow under the authority of Christ.

FROM PROMISE TO FULFILLMENT

What makes this prophecy remarkable is its progression:

1. The Command: "Sit at My right hand."
2. The Process: "Until I make…"
3. The Completion: "…your enemies your footstool."

The Father did not tell Christ to fight His enemies but to sit until the Father Himself acted. Fulfillment is God's work, not ours. Enemies may rage, but they are only hastening their own defeat. As Paul declared in 1 Corinthians 15:25, **"For he must reign, till he hath put all enemies under his feet." (KJV).**

BIBLICAL FULFILLMENT IN CHRIST

- **Peter at Pentecost** (see Acts 2:34–35): Preaching to thousands, Peter quoted Psalm 110:1 to prove that Jesus was not just a prophet but the exalted Lord. The resurrection and ascension were proof that the prophecy had come to pass.

- **Paul's Revelation** (see 1 Corinthians 15:27): Paul taught that **"He hath put all things under his feet."** Christ's victory is comprehensive—sin, Satan, and death are all defeated foes.

- **The Vision of Revelation** (see Revelation 19:16): John saw Christ returning as "KING OF KINGS AND LORD OF LORDS." The prophetic word reaches its climax when every knee bows, and every tongue confesses His Lordship.

WHAT THIS MEANS FOR US

Believers live in the tension of prophecy fulfilled and prophecy unfolding. The cross and resurrection secured victory, yet we still await the final day when death itself, the last enemy, will be destroyed (see 1 Corinthians 15:26). Until then, we live confidently knowing the outcome is settled.

Every battle you face is already written into prophecy's script: the enemy ends up under Christ's feet. Your life is not an uncertain story—it is part of a prophetic fulfillment. You are not fighting toward victory; you are living out victory already decreed in heaven.

APPLICATION POINTS

1. **The Victory Is Already Written** – I may not see the fulfillment yet, but God's Word guarantees it. I live by faith in what is promised, not fear of what is present.

2. **God Fulfills His Word** – What He spoke in Psalm 110 was fulfilled in Acts 2. What He has spoken over my life will also come to pass. His Word cannot return void.

3. **My Enemies Have an Appointment With Defeat** – Opposition may rise, but every enemy already has a place under Christ's feet. Their end is certain.

REFLECTION

- Do you believe that your present enemies are already part of Christ's prophetic victory?

- How does knowing the end of the story change the way you face battles today?

- Are you waiting in confidence or worrying in doubt while God fulfills His Word?

PRAYER

Lord, thank You for the prophetic word that all enemies are under the feet of Christ. Strengthen my faith to live in the reality of this victory, even when I face battles that seem overwhelming. Teach me to rest in Your promise, knowing that You are faithful to bring it to pass. I declare today that every enemy I face will bow before the authority of Jesus Christ. Amen.

Part II

The Call to Rest and Trust

Chapter Four

Seated in Heavenly Places with Christ

"And hath raised us up together, and made us sit together in heavenly places in Christ Jesus." — Ephesians 2:6 (KJV)

THE BELIEVER'S POSITION IN CHRIST

When Paul wrote to the Ephesian church, he gave them a startling revelation: believers are not merely forgiven or saved from sin, but raised and seated with Christ in heavenly places. This is not a future hope but a present reality. The moment we are united with Christ by faith, we share in His victory and His exaltation.

Too often, Christians live as though they are still chained to the ground of defeat. But in God's perspective, you are not beneath circumstances—you are above them. You are not struggling to gain access to heaven's authority—you are already seated in it. The throne of Christ is not only His resting place but ours as well.

THE MEANING OF BEING SEATED

To be seated speaks of completion. Jesus sat down at the right hand of the Father because His redemptive work was finished (see

Hebrews 10:12). In the same way, believers sit with Him to signify that salvation is not our work but His. We do not fight for acceptance, strive for approval, or labor for victory. We sit because the work is done.

Seating also implies shared authority. Just as an heir sits beside a king to learn rulership, so we sit with Christ to share in His reign. Romans 8:17 calls us **"joint-heirs with Christ."** What belongs to Him, by grace, belongs to us.

THE CONTRAST: EARTHLY STRUGGLES VS. HEAVENLY POSITION

Life on earth confronts us with pain, trials, and enemies. Yet, while our feet may walk dusty roads, our spirits are enthroned in heavenly places. This tension requires faith. The devil will always try to drag your mind down to earthly fear, but your spirit must rise to heavenly truth.

Paul captured this tension in Colossians 3:2–3: **"Set your affection on things above, not on things on the earth. For ye are dead, and your life is hid with Christ in God." (KJV).** We live in two realms, but victory comes when we let our heavenly seat dictate how we walk through earthly storms.

BIBLICAL EXAMPLES OF ELEVATED POSITION

- **Elisha and the Servant** (see 2 Kings 6:15–17): When surrounded by an enemy army, Elisha prayed for his servant's eyes to be opened. Suddenly, the servant saw the heavenly chariots of fire surrounding them. Though the earthly battle was real, the heavenly position was greater.

- **Stephen's Vision** (see Acts 7:55–56): As Stephen faced martyrdom, he looked up and saw Jesus standing at the right hand of God. Earthly persecution was under him because heavenly authority was over him.

- **Christ's Words** (see Luke 10:19): **"Behold, I give unto you power to tread on serpents and scorpions, and over all the power of the enemy: and nothing shall by any means hurt you." (KJV).** This is not earthly boasting but heavenly positioning.

APPLICATION POINTS

1. **My Position Determines My Perspective** – I don't see life from the valley of fear but from the throne of victory.

2. **I Am Already Victorious in Christ** – I am not fighting to win; I am enforcing a victory already secured at the cross.

3. **I Must Live From Above, Not Below** – My thoughts, prayers, and actions must reflect my heavenly seat, not my earthly struggle.

REFLECTION

- Do you live more from your earthly situation or your heavenly position?

- How would your daily battles look different if you believed you were already seated in victory?

- Are you striving for what Christ has already finished, or resting in what He has already done?

PRAYER

Father, thank You for raising me up and seating me with Christ in heavenly places. Forgive me for living as though I am beneath my battles when You have already placed me above them. Open my eyes to see life from Your throne, not from my fears. Teach me to rest in Christ's finished work and to walk in the authority You have given me. In Jesus' name. Amen.

Chapter Five

The Posture of Rest in the Midst of Battle

"The Lord will fight for you, and you have only to be silent." — Exodus 14:14 (ESV)

REST IS NOT THE ABSENCE OF BATTLE

To be seated with Christ does not mean life will be free from conflict. Scripture is clear that we wrestle against spiritual powers, face trials of many kinds, and endure seasons of testing. Yet God calls us to a posture of rest in the midst of battle. Rest is not denial of reality; it is confidence in God's ability.

When Israel stood before the Red Sea with Pharaoh's army behind them, fear filled their hearts. But Moses spoke the word of the Lord: **"The Lord will fight for you, and you have only to be silent."** In other words: stay calm, stay still, stay seated in trust because God Himself was about to act.

REST AS A WEAPON

The enemy thrives on chaos, fear, and panic. When believers remain at peace, they disarm the enemy's strategy. Isaiah 26:3 promises: **"Thou wilt keep him in perfect peace, whose mind is stayed on**

thee: because he trusteth in thee." (KJV). Peace becomes a weapon that frustrates the adversary and magnifies God's authority.

Rest is not passivity; it is active faith. It means praying instead of panicking, worshiping instead of worrying, and trusting instead of striving. It is confidence that the battle is the Lord's, not ours.

JESUS: THE PERFECT EXAMPLE OF REST

- **Sleeping in the Storm** (see Mark 4:38): When the disciples panicked in the storm, Jesus was asleep in the boat. His rest was not indifference but authority. By speaking **"Peace, be still,"** He revealed that rest precedes victory.

- **Silent Before Pilate** (see Matthew 27:14): Jesus did not argue or defend Himself in the face of false accusations. His silence demonstrated that He trusted the Father's plan more than man's judgment.

- **The Finished Work** (see Hebrews 10:12): After His sacrifice, Christ "sat down"—the ultimate posture of rest, because the greatest battle was already won.

BIBLICAL ILLUSTRATIONS OF REST IN BATTLE

- **Jehoshaphat** (see 2 Chronicles 20): Surrounded by enemies, Judah was instructed to stand still and see the salvation of the Lord. Their weapon was worship, not warfare, and God brought confusion to their enemies.

- **Daniel in the Lions' Den** (see Daniel 6): Daniel did not pace or panic; he rested in God's protection. His trust shut the mouths of lions.

- **Paul and Silas in Prison** (see Acts 16): At midnight, instead of despairing, Paul and Silas prayed and sang hymns. Their posture of rest through praise shook the prison doors open.

APPLICATION POINTS

1. **Rest is the Highest Form of Faith** – When I choose rest, I declare that I believe God more than the battle around me.

2. **My Peace Frustrates the Enemy** – Panic gives the enemy ground; peace forces him to flee.

3. **Rest Prepares Me to See God's Salvation** – When I step back, God steps in. My silence often makes space for His power.

REFLECTION

- When you face battles, do you panic or rest?

- How can you replace striving with trust in your current situation?

- Are you willing to let God fight for you instead of trying to control the outcome?

PRAYER

Father, teach me to rest, even in the midst of my greatest battles. Help me to trust that You are fighting for me when I cannot fight for myself. Let my heart be anchored in peace, my mind fixed on Your promises, and my spirit confident in Your victory. May my posture of rest glorify You and silence the enemy. In Jesus' name. Amen.

Chapter Six

Trusting God's Timing for Vindication

"For the vision is yet for an appointed time, but at the end it shall speak, and not lie: though it tarry, wait for it; because it will surely come, it will not tarry." — Habakkuk 2:3 (KJV)

THE CHALLENGE OF WAITING

One of the hardest commands in the Christian walk is to wait. We live in a world that demands instant results, but the kingdom of God operates on divine timing. Vindication—God's act of proving His people right and delivering them from their enemies—often comes after a season of waiting.

When God told His Son, **"Sit on my right hand, until I make thine enemies thy footstool." (Hebrews 1:13 - KJV)**, the keyword was *until*. There was a process between the seating and the subduing. In that gap lies the test of trust.

GOD'S TIMING IS PERFECT

Vindication delayed is not vindication denied. God is never late; He works according to His appointed time. Ecclesiastes 3:11 reminds us: **"He hath made every thing beautiful in his time." (KJV).**

Our enemies may seem to prosper temporarily, but their apparent success is only setting the stage for God's glory to be revealed.

David, who endured years of hiding from Saul, declared in Psalm 37:7–9: **"Rest in the Lord, and wait patiently for him… Cease from anger, and forsake wrath: fret not thyself in any wise to do evil. For evildoers shall be cut off: but those that wait upon the Lord, they shall inherit the earth." (KJV).**

BIBLICAL EXAMPLES OF VINDICATION IN GOD'S TIME

- **Joseph** (see Genesis 50:20): Wrongfully accused and imprisoned, Joseph waited thirteen years before his vindication came. But when it did, it elevated him to second in command in Egypt.

- **Hannah** (see 1 Samuel 1): Mocked for her barrenness, Hannah's vindication came when God gave her Samuel, a prophet who would anoint kings.

- **Jesus** (see Philippians 2:9–11): Though humiliated and crucified, He was vindicated in resurrection and exalted with the name above every name.

THE DANGERS OF FORCING VINDICATION

When believers take matters into their own hands, they often step outside God's timing. Abraham and Sarah produced Ishmael by impatience, but the promise was Isaac. Saul lost the kingdom because he could not wait for Samuel to offer a sacrifice (see 1 Samuel 13). Impatience leads to regret; waiting leads to reward.

APPLICATION POINTS

1. **Vindication Is God's Responsibility, Not Mine** – I don't need to defend myself; God will prove me right in His time.

2. **Waiting Prepares Me for the Fulfillment** – Delay is not denial; it is development. God uses the waiting season to build my character.

3. **Impatience Brings Loss, But Patience Brings Inheritance** – If I wait on God, I inherit His promises. If I rush ahead, I forfeit His best.

REFLECTION

- Are you willing to trust God's timing, even when vindication feels delayed?

- What areas of your life reveal impatience or striving to prove yourself?

- How can you practice waiting with faith instead of frustration?

PRAYER

Father, give me the grace to wait for Your timing in every area of my life. Teach me to rest in the assurance that You are working behind the scenes, even when I cannot see it. Deliver me from impatience, and help me trust that vindication belongs to You alone. May I remain seated in faith, knowing that at the appointed time, You will bring every enemy underfoot. In Jesus' name. Amen.

Chapter Seven

The Futility of Striving in Your Own Strength

"It is vain for you to rise up early, to sit up late, to eat the bread of sorrows: for so he giveth his beloved sleep." —Psalm 127:2 (KJV)

THE TEMPTATION TO STRIVE

From the beginning, humanity has struggled with the desire to accomplish by human effort what only God can do by His power. We want to prove ourselves, defend ourselves, and fight our own battles. Yet scripture warns us that human striving is futile. It drains us of strength, fills us with anxiety, and produces fruitless labor.

When God told His Son, **"Sit at My right hand until I make Your enemies Your footstool,"** the command was clear: sit, don't strive. The victory would not come through Christ's continuous struggle but through the Father's sovereign action.

THE ILLUSION OF CONTROL

Striving makes us believe that everything depends on us: our wisdom, our effort, our ability to manipulate outcomes. But control is an illusion. Jesus reminded His followers in Matthew 6:27: **"Which of you by taking thought can add one cubit unto his stature?" (KJV).** Worry and striving never change reality; they only rob us of peace.

Trust, on the other hand, acknowledges that God is in control. He is the One who opens doors, subdues enemies, and brings vindication. To strive is to doubt His sovereignty; to rest is to honor it.

BIBLICAL WARNINGS AGAINST STRIVING

- **Abraham and Sarah** (see Genesis 16): Impatience led them to strive in the flesh, producing Ishmael instead of waiting for God's promised Isaac. Their striving created generational conflict.

- **King Saul** (see 1 Samuel 13): In fear and impatience, Saul offered a sacrifice without Samuel. His striving cost him the kingdom.

- **Martha** (see Luke 10:40–42): Distracted with much serving, Martha grew frustrated while Mary chose rest at Jesus' feet. Jesus declared Mary's posture as the "better part."

JESUS: THE MODEL OF NON-STRIVING

Jesus never strove in His own strength. He healed with a word, calmed storms with a command, and cast out demons with authority. He declared in John 5:19: **"The Son can do nothing of himself, but what he seeth the Father do." (KJV).** His secret was dependence, not striving. If the sinless Son of God lived in full reliance on the Father, how much more must we?

APPLICATION POINTS

1. **Striving Produces Ishmaels, Not Isaacs** – When I force outcomes in my own strength, I create problems. God's promises only come by His power, not my effort.

2. **Rest Honors God's Sovereignty** – Trusting instead of striving is an act of worship. It declares that God is in control, not me.

3. **God Works While I Rest** – As Psalm 127:2 reminds us, God gives His beloved sleep. Rest is not wasted time; it is sacred trust.

REFLECTION

- In what areas of your life are you still striving instead of sitting?

- Are you producing Ishmaels because you are unwilling to wait for God's promise?

- How can you shift from anxious effort to confident trust in God's ability?

PRAYER

Father, forgive me for the times I have strived in my own strength instead of trusting in Your power. Deliver me from the illusion of control, and teach me to rest in Your sovereignty. Help me to sit at Your feet, knowing that You are faithful to bring every promise to pass. May my life reflect dependence on You, not on myself. In Jesus' name. Amen.

Part III

God's Process of Victory

Chapter Eight

God's Strategy of Delay: Why He Says "Wait"

"The Lord is not slack concerning his promise, as some men count slackness; but is longsuffering to us-ward, not willing that any should perish, but that all should come to repentance." — 2 Peter 3:9 (KJV)

THE MYSTERY OF DIVINE DELAY

Waiting is one of the most difficult aspects of the Christian journey. We pray, we believe, and yet God often tells us to wait. At first glance, delay looks like denial, but in God's kingdom, delay is strategy. He never withholds victory to discourage us; He delays to prepare us and to magnify His glory.

When the Father told the Son, **"Sit at My right hand, til I make Your enemies Your footstool" (Hebrews 1:13 - NKJV)**, the key word again is *until*. That little word holds the mystery of delay. Christ sat while the Father worked out the process of bringing every enemy underfoot. The waiting was not wasted; it was purposeful.

WHY GOD DELAYS

1. **To Develop Character** – David was anointed king as a teenager, but did not ascend the throne until years later. The delay built endurance, humility, and dependence on God. Without the wilderness, David could not handle the palace.

2. **To Increase Dependence** – Paul prayed three times for the thorn in his flesh to be removed, but God's answer was, **"My grace is sufficient for thee" (2 Corinthians 12:9 - KJV).** Delay shifted Paul's focus from self-sufficiency to God's sufficiency.

3. **To Demonstrate His Glory** – Jesus delayed going to Lazarus until after he had died, so that the miracle of resurrection would reveal the glory of God (see John 11:4–6). Had He come sooner, they would have seen a healing, but because of delay, they witnessed resurrection power.

4. **To Align with His Perfect Timing** – Habakkuk 2:3 reminds us: **"Though it tarry, wait for it; because it will surely come, it will not tarry." (KJV).** What looks like slowness to us is perfect timing to God.

THE DANGER OF RESISTING DELAY

When believers refuse to accept God's timing, they often sabotage their destiny. Abraham and Sarah's impatience produced Ishmael, creating generational conflict. Saul's refusal to wait cost him the kingdom (see 1 Samuel 13). Delay is a test, not to weaken us but to prove us. Passing the test means inheriting the promise; failing the test means forfeiting it.

BIBLICAL ILLUSTRATIONS OF STRATEGIC DELAY

- **Israel in Egypt** (see Exodus 12): God waited 400 years before delivering Israel, not because He forgot, but because He was fulfilling prophecy and preparing them for freedom.

- **Jesus' Ministry** (see Luke 3:23): The Son of God waited thirty years before beginning His public ministry. Delay was not wasted; it was preparation.

- **Pentecost** (see Acts 1:4): The disciples were told to wait in Jerusalem until the Holy Spirit came. That delay birthed the greatest outpouring in history.

APPLICATION POINTS

1. **Delay Is Part of God's Design** – I will not despise waiting; I will see it as preparation for destiny.

2. **What Looks Like Pause Is Really Process** – God is aligning people, timing, and circumstances for His glory.

3. **If I Rush, I Risk** – Impatience may lead me to forfeit blessings. Trusting God's timing ensures His best.

REFLECTION

- Do you view delay as punishment or preparation?

- What lessons is God teaching you in your current season of waiting?

- Are you willing to sit in trust until God brings the promise to pass?

PRAYER

Father, thank You for the wisdom of delay. Forgive me for the times I have grown impatient and tried to force outcomes in my own strength. Help me to see waiting as part of Your divine strategy, not as a denial of Your promise. Give me grace to remain seated in faith until You bring every enemy underfoot. I trust Your timing, knowing it is always perfect. In Jesus' name. Amen.

Chapter Nine

The Making of a Footstool: Enemies Becoming Platforms

"But as for you, ye thought evil against me; but God meant it unto good, to bring to pass, as it is this day, to save much people alive." — Genesis 50:20 (KJV)

THE FOOTSTOOL PRINCIPLE

When God promised to make Christ's enemies His footstool (see Hebrews 1:13), He revealed a profound principle: the very opposition we face becomes the platform for our promotion. A footstool, by design, lifts a person higher. Likewise, enemies do not stop the believer's destiny, they elevate it.

Joseph declared this truth to his brothers: **"You meant evil against me; but God meant it for good" (see Genesis 50:20).** What they intended to destroy him only positioned him for greater authority. The betrayal became a footstool. The pit, the prison, and the false accusations all aligned to raise him to the palace.

ENEMIES AS STEPPING STONES

God never wastes opposition. Every enemy is a potential stepping stone in His plan.

- Goliath was not David's downfall but his footstool. Had there been no giant, there would have been no throne.

- Pharaoh was not Israel's end but their footstool. His resistance magnified God's power in the plagues and the Red Sea deliverance.

- The cross was not Christ's defeat but His footstool. What looked like loss became the greatest victory in history.

In each case, opposition did not hinder destiny, it propelled it.

THE MAKING OF A FOOTSTOOL IN YOUR LIFE

Your greatest enemies may be the very instruments God uses to elevate you. The betrayal that broke your heart, the job you lost, the sickness that seemed unbearable—in God's hands, these become platforms for His glory. Romans 8:28 assures us: **"…all things work together for good to them that love God, to them who are the called according to his purpose." (KJV).**

This does not mean the enemy's actions are good, but it does mean God has the power to turn them into good. The devil intends destruction, but God transforms it into elevation.

BIBLICAL EXAMPLES OF FOOTSTOOL MOMENTS

- **Moses and Pharaoh** (see Exodus 14): Pharaoh's stubbornness positioned Moses to lead Israel through the Red Sea. His resistance became the stage for God's deliverance.

- **Daniel and His Accusers** (see Daniel 6): The plot to destroy Daniel ended with his promotion. The lion's den became his footstool.

- **Paul and His Chains** (see Philippians 1:12–13): Paul's imprisonment advanced the gospel, making his chains a platform for the message of Christ.

APPLICATION POINTS

1. **My Enemies Are My Elevators** – What looks like opposition is often God's setup for promotion.

2. **The Cross Precedes the Crown** – Before every throne there is always a footstool. I must not despise what God is using to raise me.

3. **God Transforms Pain Into Platforms** – No wound is wasted. Every trial becomes a testimony.

REFLECTION

- Are you seeing your enemies as obstacles or as stepping stones?

- What past battle in your life has God already turned into a footstool?

- How can you shift your perspective to see present struggles as platforms for God's glory?

PRAYER

Father, thank You that my enemies cannot stop my destiny but only serve to elevate me into Your plan. Open my eyes to see opposition as opportunity, and trials as platforms for testimony. Teach me to trust that You are turning every weapon formed against me into a footstool beneath my feet. May my life reflect the power of Your sovereignty and the beauty of Your redemption. In Jesus' name. Amen.

Chapter Ten

From Opposition to Elevation

"So the last shall be first, and the first last: for many be called, but few chosen." — Matthew 20:16 (KJV)

THE GOD OF REVERSALS

One of the great themes of scripture is God's ability to reverse situations. He takes the least and makes them the greatest, the rejected and makes them chosen, the oppressed and makes them rulers. Divine reversals are God's way of proving that His sovereignty rules over human schemes.

What man intends for harm, God flips for good. What the enemy designs for destruction, God uses for promotion. This is not coincidence, it is kingdom principle.

"He raiseth up the poor out of the dust, and lifteth up the beggar from the dunghill, to set them among princes." (1 Samuel 2:8 - KJV).

REVERSALS IN SCRIPTURE

- **Joseph** (see Genesis 41:41–43): Betrayed by his brothers, sold as a slave, and imprisoned by lies, yet God reversed it all, making him ruler of Egypt.

- **Esther** (see Esther 9:1): Haman's plot to destroy the Jews turned back on his own head. The day appointed for Israel's destruction became the day of their deliverance.

- **Daniel** (see Daniel 6:23–28): Accused and cast into the lions' den, Daniel emerged unharmed, while his accusers faced the very fate they designed for him. His opposition led to his elevation.

- **Jesus** (see Philippians 2:8–9): Crucified in shame, buried in weakness, yet God highly exalted Him, giving Him the name above every name.

WHY GOD USES REVERSALS

1. **To Display His Glory** – Only God can take death and turn it into resurrection, or turn a cross into a throne. Reversals magnify His power.

2. **To Humble the Proud and Exalt the Humble** – God resists the proud but gives grace to the humble (see James 4:6). Reversals realign human pride with divine justice.

3. **To Advance His Kingdom Purposes** – What seems like a setback in the natural often advances God's will in the

spiritual. Paul's imprisonment, for example, spread the gospel further (see Philippians 1:12–13).

THE BELIEVER'S CONFIDENCE IN REVERSALS

When you face opposition, you must remember: it is not the end of the story. The God of reversals is still at work. He has promised: **"No weapon that is formed against thee shall prosper." (Isaiah 54:17 - KJV).** The very schemes designed to defeat you are the instruments God will use to elevate you.

Your rejection today may be the stage for your promotion tomorrow. Your opposition today may become the evidence of God's favor tomorrow. God has a way of flipping the script so that His glory is revealed and His people are lifted.

APPLICATION POINTS

1. **What the Enemy Meant for Evil, God Will Turn for Good** – Every plot against me is already being rewritten for my promotion.

2. **My Delay Is Not Denial; It Is Setup for Reversal** – The longer the wait, the greater the testimony.

3. **Rejection Is Not the End; It Is Often the Door to Elevation** – God uses human rejection as a pathway to divine selection.

REFLECTION

- What situation in your life seems impossible to reverse right now?

- How has God already reversed past opposition into elevation for you?

- Are you trusting God to flip your current trial into triumph, or are you still doubting His power?

PRAYER

Father, I thank You that You are the God of divine reversals. What the enemy meant for my destruction, You are turning into my elevation. I choose to trust You when I face opposition, knowing that You can flip every trial into triumph and every setback into a setup for promotion. Let my life be a testimony that You raise the lowly and exalt the humble. In Jesus' name. Amen.

Chapter Eleven

Lessons from David's Throne and Saul's Spear

"And Saul cast the javelin; for he said, I will smite David even to the wall with it. And David avoided out of his presence twice." — 1 Samuel 18:11 (KJV)

THE PATHWAY TO THE THRONE

David was anointed as king while still a shepherd boy (see 1 Samuel 16), but his journey to the throne was anything but smooth. Though chosen by God, he endured years of rejection, pursuit, and attempted murder at the hand of King Saul. Instead of immediate elevation, David faced spears.

Why would God allow this? Because the throne requires more than anointing; it requires character. Spears test integrity. Opposition tests obedience. Before David could wear the crown, he had to learn how to handle the spear without picking it up himself.

SAUL'S SPEARS: THE TEST OF CHARACTER

Saul's jealousy of David caused him to hurl spears in an attempt to kill him. Twice, David could have retaliated, but he chose restraint.

59

He refused to return spear for spear. Instead, he honored Saul as God's anointed, even while being pursued as an enemy.

This reveals a powerful lesson: how we handle spears determines if we are ready for the throne. Many disqualify themselves from greater authority because they cannot resist the urge to retaliate. David's refusal to strike back positioned him for elevation.

THRONE LESSONS FROM DAVID'S JOURNEY

1. **The Throne Comes Through the Wilderness** – David spent years hiding in caves, learning dependence on God. The wilderness was not wasted; it was preparation.

2. **The Throne Requires Humility** – Twice David had the chance to kill Saul (see 1 Samuel 24, 26), but he refused, declaring: **"I will not put forth mine hand against my lord; for he is the Lord's anointed."** His humility secured his destiny.

3. **The Throne Demands God's Timing** – David waited patiently for God to remove Saul. He trusted God's process instead of forcing the crown. His restraint showed he understood: what God anoints, only God can remove.

THE SPEAR IN OUR LIVES

All believers will face "Saul's spears" at some point—attacks, betrayals, false accusations, or jealousy from others. These spears are not sent to destroy us but to shape us. How we respond reveals whether we are ready for greater authority.

- If we pick up the spear and retaliate, we step out of God's will.

- If we avoid the spear and trust God's timing, we step into destiny.

APPLICATION POINTS

1. **Spears Are Tests, Not Final Defeats** – The enemy's attack is not the end; it is preparation for promotion.

2. **The Throne Belongs to the Patient** – Waiting on God's timing instead of forcing outcomes proves we are ready for His promise.

3. **Character Qualifies Us for the Crown** – Anointing opens the door, but character keeps us seated on the throne.

REFLECTION

- How are you handling the "spears" being thrown at you right now?

- Are you tempted to retaliate, or are you trusting God's timing for vindication?

- What lessons from David's restraint can you apply to your own battles?

PRAYER

Father, help me to handle the spears of life with grace and faith. Teach me to resist retaliation and to trust Your timing for elevation. Shape my character in the wilderness so I am prepared for the throne You have prepared for me. May I honor even in hardship, remain faithful in trial, and wait patiently for Your perfect plan. In Jesus' name. Amen.

Part IV

Living in Triumph

Chapter Twelve

When the Lord Fights Your Battles

"The Lord shall fight for you, and ye shall hold your peace." — Exodus 14:14 (KJV)

THE GOD WHO FIGHTS FOR HIS PEOPLE

Throughout scripture, God reveals Himself as the Warrior who fights on behalf of His people. Israel stood at the Red Sea with Pharaoh's army closing in, terrified and helpless. Yet Moses declared, **"The Lord shall fight for you."** The battle was not Israel's to win, it was God's. He split the sea, drowned their enemies, and established His people's victory without them lifting a sword.

This same God has not changed. He is still the One who fights for His children. Believers are not left to struggle in their own strength but are called to rest in the assurance that the Lord Himself engages the enemy on their behalf.

WHY THE LORD FIGHTS FOR US

1. **Because the Battle Belongs to Him – "For the battle is not yours, but God's" (2 Chronicles 20:15 - KJV).** When enemies rise against us, they are ultimately rising against

God's plan and God's people. He takes ownership of the fight.

2. **Because We Are His Covenant People** – Just as God defended Israel, He defends all who belong to Him. His covenant of protection ensures that no weapon formed against us shall prosper (see Isaiah 54:17).

3. **Because Our Strength Is Not Enough** – God allows battles beyond our ability to remind us that victory comes only through His power. Paul declared, **"When I am weak, then am I strong." (2 Corinthians 12:10 - KJV).**

BIBLICAL EXAMPLES OF GOD FIGHTING FOR HIS PEOPLE

- **Jehoshaphat and Judah** (see 2 Chronicles 20): Surrounded by vast armies, Judah fasted, prayed, and worshiped. God caused confusion among their enemies, and they destroyed one another without Judah needing to fight.

- **David and Goliath** (see 1 Samuel 17): David declared, **"the battle is the Lord's"** (see 1 Samuel 17:47). His victory over Goliath was not by sword or spear but by faith in God's power.

- **Hezekiah and Assyria** (see 2 Kings 19): When the Assyrian King threatened Jerusalem, Hezekiah prayed. That night, the angel of the Lord struck down 185,000 soldiers. God fought without Israel drawing a weapon.

HOW GOD FIGHTS TODAY

God may not always part seas or send angels visibly, but He still fights:

- He fights through His Word, which is a sword against the enemy's lies.

- He fights through His Spirit, who intercedes for us when we cannot pray (see Romans 8:26).

- He fights through His providence, arranging circumstances for our deliverance.

- He fights through His Son, who already conquered sin, death, and the grave.

APPLICATION POINTS

1. **I Can Rest Because the Battle Is the Lord's** – I don't need to carry what God has already claimed as His fight.

2. **My Worship Is My Weapon** – Just as Judah worshiped and God fought, I can praise my way into victory.

3. **Victory Is Guaranteed Because of Who Fights for Me** – If God is for me, no enemy can stand against me (see Romans 8:31).

REFLECTION

- Are you trying to fight battles in your own strength that belong to the Lord?

- Do you trust God's ability enough to rest in His promise?

- How can you use worship and prayer as weapons instead of worry and fear?

PRAYER

Lord, thank You that You are the Warrior who fights on my behalf. Forgive me for the times I have tried to handle battles in my own strength. I surrender every fight into Your hands today. Teach me to rest in Your power, to worship in the face of opposition, and to trust that You will bring victory. May every enemy see that the battle is Yours and the glory belongs to You. In Jesus' name. Amen.

Chapter Thirteen

Your Enemies as Stepping Stones to Destiny

"Thou preparest a table before me in the presence of mine enemies." — Psalm 23:5 (KJV)

ENEMIES HAVE A PURPOSE IN DESTINY

Enemies do not appear in our lives by accident. While their intentions may be to harm, God uses them to position, strengthen, and propel His children into purpose. Joseph told his brothers, **"...ye thought evil against me; but God meant it unto good" (Genesis 50:20 - KJV).** What they designed for destruction became the very path to Joseph's destiny.

God doesn't waste battles. Every enemy that rises is transformed by His power into a stepping stone, not to push you down but to lift you higher.

BIBLICAL PATTERNS OF ENEMIES AS STEPPING STONES

- **Joseph's Brothers** → Path to the Palace - His betrayal became the gateway to Egypt, where he rose to govern nations and save lives.

- **David's Goliath** → Path to the Throne - Goliath wasn't an obstacle but a divine opportunity. Killing the giant positioned David for recognition and honor, setting him on the road to kingship.

- **Esther's Haman** → Path to Royal Influence - Haman plotted genocide, but God turned his schemes into Esther's moment of courage and deliverance for her people.

- **Jesus' Cross** → Path to Resurrection - The cross was meant for shame and defeat, yet it became the stepping stone to the greatest victory in history—resurrection and eternal redemption.

HOW ENEMIES BECOME STEPPING STONES

1. **They Expose What God Has Placed Inside You** – Without Goliath, David's anointing as a warrior would not have been revealed.

2. **They Push You Out of Comfort Zones** – Joseph would never have left home for Egypt without betrayal forcing him forward.

3. **They Become Platforms for God's Glory** – When enemies rise, they create a stage for God to demonstrate His power publicly.

4. **They Build Spiritual Maturity** – Trials strengthen character, endurance, and faith that could not be developed in ease.

APPLICATION POINTS

- I must see enemies as opportunities for elevation, not destruction.

- God uses resistance to refine and redirect my steps toward destiny.

- If I respond in faith, every opposition becomes part of my promotion.

REFLECTION

- Are you focusing more on the attack of enemies or the advancement God is bringing through them?

- What recent opposition might actually be God's stepping stone for your growth?

- How can you shift your perspective from fear of enemies to faith in God's purpose?

PRAYER

Father, thank You for turning every enemy into a stepping stone toward my destiny. Teach me to see through the eyes of faith when opposition rises. Help me not to fear the schemes of the enemy but to embrace them as opportunities for growth and promotion. Like Joseph, David, Esther, and Jesus, may I recognize that what the enemy meant for evil, You are working for my good. In Jesus' name. Amen.

Chapter Fourteen

Walking in Confidence, Not Fear

"For God hath not given us the spirit of fear; but of power, and of love, and of a sound mind." — 2 Timothy 1:7 (KJV)

FEAR: THE ENEMY OF VICTORY

Fear has always been one of the enemy's greatest weapons. It paralyzes, blinds, and causes us to doubt the promises of God. Fear whispers lies that God will not come through, that enemies are too great, and that the throne of Christ is not enough to secure victory.

But fear is not from God. The Lord has not given His children a spirit of fear but has clothed us with power, love, and a sound mind. If we are seated with Christ, fear has no legal right to control us.

CONFIDENCE ROOTED IN CHRIST

Walking in confidence does not mean arrogance or pride—it means being anchored in Christ's finished work. Confidence says:

- *"I know who I am in Christ."*
- *"I know whose authority I carry."*

- *"I know my enemies are under my feet."*

The early church faced persecution, imprisonment, and even death, yet they declared the Word with boldness. Their confidence came not from circumstances but from Christ's throne.

BIBLICAL EXAMPLES OF CONFIDENCE IN GOD

- **David Before Goliath** – David did not boast in his sling but in the name of the Lord of Hosts (see 1 Samuel 17:45).

- **Daniel in the Lions' Den** – He faced the threat of death with unshakable faith, knowing God's power to deliver (see Daniel 6:22).

- **The Apostles Before the Sanhedrin** – When commanded to be silent, Peter and John declared, **"...we cannot but speak the things which we have seen and heard." (Acts 4:20 - KJV).**

- **Paul in Prison** – Even in chains, Paul declared, **"I know whom I have believed" (2 Timothy 1:12 - KJV).**

Each of these men walked in confidence, not because of who they were, but because of who God is.

HOW TO WALK IN CONFIDENCE, NOT FEAR

1. **Renew Your Mind with the Word** – Fear thrives on lies. Confidence grows when we believe what God has spoken.

2. **Pray Bold Prayers** – Prayer is not timid begging; it is declaring God's will in faith, knowing He hears us.

3. **Guard Your Identity** – Fear tries to make you forget you are a child of God. Confidence flows from knowing you are seated with Christ.

4. **Stand in Love – "…perfect love casteth out fear" (1 John 4:18 - KJV).** Confidence grows when love, not fear, motivates our actions.

5. **Remember God's Track Record** – Reflecting on past victories strengthens present faith. The God who delivered before will deliver again.

PRACTICAL APPLICATIONS

- I must stop rehearsing the enemy's lies and start declaring God's truth.

- Fear loses its power when I fix my eyes on the throne, not the threat.

- Confidence means stepping forward in obedience, even when I don't see the outcome.

- My boldness is not in myself but in Christ, who reigns forever.

REFLECTION

- What fears have you allowed to silence your faith or delay your obedience?

- How can you cultivate bold confidence rooted in Christ's authority?

- Do you live as though fear is greater than faith, or do you live seated in victory?

PROPHETIC DECLARATION

I declare that I will no longer walk in fear, for fear is not my portion. I am clothed with power, love, and a sound mind. I walk in holy boldness, declaring God's Word and living in kingdom authority. My confidence is in Christ alone, and because He reigns, I will not be shaken.

CLOSING PRAYER

Father, I thank You that fear is broken by the power of Your Spirit. I reject the lies of the enemy and embrace the truth of who I am in Christ. Clothe me with boldness, fill me with courage, and help me to walk in confidence every day. Let my life reflect Your victory, and may others be drawn to You through my faith. In Jesus' name. Amen.

Chapter Fifteen

From Seated to Reigning: Sharing in His Authority

"And hath raised us up together, and made us sit together in heavenly places in Christ Jesus." — Ephesians 2:6 (KJV)

SEATED WITH CHRIST

When Christ ascended, He did not sit alone at the right hand of the Father; He brought His people with Him. Scripture says we are **"raised up together"** and **"seated together with Him."** This is more than a future hope in heaven; it is a present reality of spiritual position.

To be seated with Christ means:

- I am no longer striving for acceptance—I am already accepted.

- I am no longer bound under sin—I am already free.

- I am no longer beneath the enemy's power—I am already above.

Seating speaks of rest, authority, and permanence. Just as a king sits on his throne to rule, so believers sit with Christ to reign.

FROM POSITION TO PRACTICE

Though we are spiritually seated with Christ, many believers live as though they are still defeated. The challenge is not our position but our perception. We must move from knowing we are seated to living as though we are reigning.

- **Position:** Seated with Christ.
- **Practice:** Walking in His authority.
- **Purpose:** Reigning with Him over the works of darkness.

The throne is not a decorative symbol—it is a place of government, dominion, and decision-making. God has invited us to share in His Son's authority and carry His kingdom into the earth.

SHARING IN CHRIST'S AUTHORITY

1. Authority Over Sin

Romans 6:14a declares, **"For sin shall not have dominion over you." (KJV)**. Sharing in Christ's authority means sin no longer rules our lives. We walk in holiness, not by striving, but by the power of the Spirit.

2. Authority Over Satan

Luke 10:19 reminds us: **"Behold, I give unto you power to tread on serpents and scorpions, and over all the power of the** enemy." **(KJV).** Authority means Satan is not our equal opponent but a defeated foe under our feet.

3. Authority in Prayer

When we pray in Jesus' name, we are not making empty requests but issuing decrees backed by heaven's throne. Binding and loosing are not symbolic, they are real spiritual transactions (see Matthew 18:18).

4. Authority in Kingdom Assignment

Reigning with Christ is not passive. It means exercising dominion in our God-given spheres—homes, communities, ministries, and nations—until the kingdoms of this world become the kingdom of our Lord and His Christ (see Revelation 11:15).

THE PROCESS OF REIGNING

1. **Identity** – Know who you are: a son/daughter of the King.

2. **Submission** – Authority flows from alignment. To reign with Christ, we must remain submitted to Christ.

3. **Boldness** – Reigning requires courage to speak, act, and declare God's truth without fear.

4. **Faithfulness** – Jesus said, **"If we suffer, we shall also reign with him" (2 Timothy 2:12 - KJV).** Our reigning begins with endurance in the present.

PRACTICAL APPLICATIONS

- I must stop living as a beggar when God has called me to reign as royalty.

- Every challenge is not proof of defeat but an invitation to exercise authority.

- To reign with Christ is to release His will in the earth through prayer, obedience, and bold action.

- My throne is not in the future only—it is my reality now in Christ.

REFLECTION

- Do you live from the posture of being seated with Christ, or do you still act as if you are beneath the enemy's power?

- In what areas of your life do you need to step into Christ's authority?

- How can you better align your daily practice with your eternal position?

PROPHETIC DECLARATION

I declare that I am seated with Christ in heavenly places. I reign with Him in authority, power, and victory. Sin shall not have dominion over me. Satan is under my feet. I walk in boldness, releasing the kingdom of God into every area of my life. I will no longer live as a victim, for I am called to reign as a king and priest in Christ Jesus.

CLOSING PRAYER

Father, thank You for raising me up and seating me with Christ in heavenly places. Help me not only to rest in this position but to reign from it. Teach me to exercise Your authority in my prayers, in my walk, and in my witness. May my life reflect the rule of Christ until every enemy is made His footstool. In Jesus' name. Amen.

Part V

Eternal Victory

Chapter Sixteen

The Final Enemy: Death Under His Feet

"The last enemy that shall be destroyed is death." — 1 Corinthians 15:26 (KJV)

THE CERTAINTY OF DEATH'S DEFEAT

From the beginning of human history, death has loomed as humanity's greatest enemy. It silenced prophets, ended kings, and brought grief to families. Yet scripture reveals a greater truth: death is not eternal, and its reign is temporary. Paul declared with confidence that death itself will one day be completely destroyed.

Jesus has already conquered death through His resurrection. At the empty tomb, the sting of death was broken, and its victory was annulled. Still, its final destruction will come at the end of time when Christ establishes His eternal kingdom and death is swallowed up forever.

CHRIST'S VICTORY OVER DEATH

1. **At the Cross** – By dying in our place, Christ disarmed the power of sin and removed the curse that leads to death (see Colossians 2:14–15).

85

2. **In the Grave** – For three days, death tried to hold Him, but the grave could not keep the Lord of Life.

3. **In Resurrection** – Christ rose with authority, declaring, **"I am he that liveth, and was dead; and, behold, I am alive for evermore, Amen; and have the keys of hell and of death." (Revelation 1:18 - KJV).**

Because of His victory, death is no longer a prison for the believer but a doorway into eternal life.

THE FINAL JUDGMENT OF DEATH

Revelation 20:14 describes the climactic moment: **"And death and hell were cast into the lake of fire. This is the second death." (KJV).** Death itself—that ancient enemy—will be thrown away forever. Imagine it: no more funerals, no more mourning, no more graves, no more goodbyes.

This is why Paul could taunt death with boldness:

"O death, where is thy sting? O grave, where is thy victory?" (1 Corinthians 15:55 - KJV).

The resurrection turns the funeral dirge into a song of triumph.

IMPLICATIONS FOR BELIEVERS

- **We Do Not Fear Death** – For the believer, death has lost its terror. To die is gain (see Philippians 1:21).

- **We Grieve with Hope** – When loved ones in Christ pass away, we weep, but not as those without hope (see 1 Thessalonians 4:13).

- **We Live with Eternity in View** – Knowing that death is defeated should shape how we live today—with urgency, holiness, and hope.

- **We Await the Resurrection** – One day, the dead in Christ shall rise first, and we who are alive shall be caught up with them (see 1 Thessalonians 4:16–17).

PRACTICAL APPLICATIONS

- I must live daily with an eternal perspective, knowing this world is not my home.

- I must refuse the fear of death, because death itself fears the resurrection.

- I must use my time wisely, winning souls while the day lasts.

- I must anchor my hope in Christ, who guarantees life after death.

REFLECTION

- Do you truly believe that death is defeated, or do you still fear it as if it holds power over you?

- How does the reality of resurrection shape the way you live today?

- In what ways can you use the time you have to leave an eternal impact for Christ?

PROPHETIC DECLARATION

I declare that death has no hold on me. Through Christ, I have eternal life, and the sting of death is broken. I will not fear the grave, for my Redeemer lives. When I close my eyes on this side, I will awaken in His presence. Death is defeated, the grave is empty, and victory belongs to Jesus. Amen.

CLOSING PRAYER

Father, thank You that the final enemy, death, is already under the feet of Christ. Thank You that my hope is secure in His resurrection. Help me to live each day with eternity in my heart, unshaken by fear, and steadfast in faith. May my life testify to the victory of Jesus, until the day I stand before Him face to face. In Jesus' name. Amen.

Chapter Seventeen

The Unshakable Kingdom and the Seated King

"Wherefore we receiving a kingdom which cannot be moved, let us have grace, whereby we may serve God acceptably with reverence and godly fear." — Hebrews 12:28 (KJV)

THE KINGDOM THAT CANNOT BE SHAKEN

Every earthly kingdom eventually falls. History is filled with the rise and collapse of empires—Babylon, Persia, Greece, Rome—each one mighty in its day, yet all reduced to ruins. But the kingdom of God is different. It is eternal, unshakable, and indestructible.

Hebrews 12 reminds us that everything that can be shaken will be shaken, but the kingdom of God will remain forever. This means no political upheaval, no cultural decay, no demonic scheme, and no worldly power can topple the reign of Christ.

THE SEATED KING

At the center of this unshakable kingdom is not a throne of man, but the throne of God. Christ, seated at the right hand of the Father, reigns with absolute authority. His throne is established in righteousness and justice (see Psalm 89:14). Unlike earthly rulers who rise and fall, Jesus reigns forever.

- **Seated in Victory** – His work is finished; His power absolute.

- **Seated in Authority** – All power in heaven and earth has been given to Him (see Matthew 28:18).

- **Seated in Glory** – Every angel, demon, and human authority must bow before Him.

When we confess Jesus as Lord, we are declaring allegiance to the King whose throne will never be shaken.

WHAT IT MEANS FOR BELIEVERS

1. **Our Faith Is Secure** – We are not building our lives on fragile foundations but on the eternal rock of Christ.

2. **Our Hope Is Unshakable** – No matter how unstable the world becomes, our hope is anchored in a kingdom that will endure.

3. **Our Allegiance Is Clear** – We do not serve temporary rulers; we serve the King of kings. This demands loyalty, obedience, and reverence.

4. **Our Future Is Certain** – While the kingdoms of this world crumble, the kingdom we belong to will outlast them all.

PRACTICAL APPLICATIONS

- I must evaluate where my trust lies—in earthly systems or in the eternal kingdom.

- When trials come, I must remind myself: everything else may shake, but Christ's throne is unshakable.

- I must live with kingdom values now, not waiting until eternity to serve my King faithfully.

- My worship, obedience, and devotion belong to the King who reigns forever.

REFLECTION

- Are you building your life on what is shakable or unshakable?

- Do you live as if Christ is truly seated and reigning, or do you let fear rule you?

- How can you reflect kingdom loyalty in a world that is constantly shifting?

PROPHETIC DECLARATION

I declare that I belong to an unshakable kingdom. Christ, the seated King, reigns over my life, family, and future. Though the world may tremble and empires may fall, His throne is eternal. I will not be moved, for my life is anchored in His reign. I serve Him with reverence, boldness, and unwavering faith. Amen.

CLOSING PRAYER

Father, thank You that I am part of a kingdom that cannot be shaken. Thank You that Jesus reigns as the seated King, victorious and eternal. Help me to live with unshakable faith in a shaking world. Teach me to trust in Your throne when everything else crumbles. May my life reflect loyalty to Your kingdom above all else. In Jesus' name. Amen.

Chapter Eighteen

The Church Victorious with Christ

"And I say also unto thee, That thou art Peter, and upon this rock I will build my church; and the gates of hell shall not prevail against it." — Matthew 16:18 (KJV)

THE CHURCH WAS BORN IN POWER

The church of Jesus Christ was not birthed in weakness but in fire. On the day of Pentecost, the Holy Spirit came upon 120 believers, filling them with boldness, authority, and power. From that moment forward, the church has been a victorious force on the earth, advancing the kingdom of God against the powers of darkness.

Jesus promised that the gates of hell would not prevail against His church. This was not a casual statement—it was a declaration of unstoppable victory. Gates are defensive structures, which means the church is not hiding in fear but advancing, breaking through every barrier the enemy sets up.

THE CHURCH'S VICTORIOUS IDENTITY

1. **The Body of Christ** – As His body, we share in His authority and victory (see 1 Corinthians 12:27). What He has conquered, we walk in.

2. **The Bride of Christ** – As His bride, we are loved, cherished, and prepared for His coming (see Ephesians 5:27). Our destiny is glory, not defeat.

3. **The Army of Christ** – As His army, we wage spiritual warfare, but we do so from a position of assured triumph (see 2 Corinthians 10:4).

4. **The Witness of Christ** – As His witnesses, we carry His gospel to the nations, tearing down strongholds and rescuing souls from darkness (see Acts 1:8).

THE VICTORIOUS CHURCH THROUGH THE AGES

From the persecuted church in Acts to underground believers in hostile nations today, the church has faced opposition, yet it has never been extinguished. Empires have tried to crush it, rulers have tried to silence it, and cultures have tried to erase it, but the church remains. Why? Because the Head of the church is alive and reigning.

Every martyr, every revival, every missionary, and every faithful saint is a testimony that the church is not fragile but victorious.

OUR ROLE IN THE VICTORY

- **To Advance, Not Retreat** – The church is called to move forward with the gospel, not hide behind walls of fear.

- **To Shine as Light** – In a dark world, the church shines as the radiant bride, reflecting Christ's glory.

- **To Stand United** – A divided church cannot fully walk in victory. Unity is essential for kingdom impact.
- **To Prepare for Eternity** – The victorious church is not only for today but for the day when Christ returns to gather His bride.

PRACTICAL APPLICATIONS

- I must view myself not as a weak Christian but as part of a victorious church.

- I must contribute to the advance of the kingdom through prayer, service, and soul-winning.

- I must walk in confidence that no scheme of hell can destroy the people of God.

- I must remember that my place in the church connects me to eternal triumph.

REFLECTION

- Do you see yourself as part of a victorious church, or have you believed the enemy's lie that we are losing?

- How are you actively helping the church advance against the gates of hell?

- In what ways can you embody the strength, love, and authority of Christ's bride in this generation?

PROPHETIC DECLARATION

I declare that I am part of a victorious church, built upon the rock of Christ. The gates of hell shall not prevail against me, my family, or the people of God. I walk in the triumph of the risen Christ, advancing His kingdom and shining His light. I am not defeated, for I am the church victorious with Christ.

CLOSING PRAYER

Lord Jesus, thank You that You are building a church that the gates of hell cannot overcome. Thank You that I am part of that glorious body, chosen and victorious in You. Empower me to serve faithfully, witness boldly, and stand in unity with my brothers and sisters. May my life contribute to the advance of Your kingdom until the day You return for Your bride. In Your mighty name. Amen.

Chapter Nineteen

Until He Comes: Living Seated in Hope

"So Christ was once offered to bear the sins of many; and unto them that look for him shall he appear the second time without sin unto salvation." — Hebrews 9:28 (KJV)

THE POSTURE OF WAITING

The Christian life is a life of expectation. We are not only looking back to the Cross where victory was secured, but looking forward to the day when Christ returns to complete what He began. Our calling is not to live in fear of the future, but in hope, seated in the assurance of His promise.

Jesus told His disciples, **"I go to prepare a place for you. And if I go and prepare a place for you, I will come again"** (see John 14:2–3). That promise fuels our faith. We are not waiting in uncertainty but resting in the certainty that He is coming again.

HOPE ANCHORED IN VICTORY

The hope of Christ's return is not wishful thinking; it is a guaranteed reality. The One who conquered sin, Satan, and death will return as the victorious King to gather His bride and establish His eternal kingdom.

This hope shapes how we live:

- We remain steadfast in trials because we know glory awaits (see Romans 8:18).

- We remain holy because we want to be found ready (see 1 John 3:3).

- We remain watchful because no man knows the day or the hour (see Matthew 24:36).

Hope is not passive; it fuels perseverance.

LIVING SEATED UNTIL HE COMES

1. **Resting in His Finished Work** – My salvation is secure. I don't strive for acceptance, I live from it.

2. **Walking in His Authority** – I am called to reign in life, exercising kingdom dominion here and now.

3. **Witnessing to the World** – Hope in His coming drives urgency in the mission. If He tarries, it is only so more souls may be saved (see 2 Peter 3:9).

4. **Enduring with Joy** – Waiting is not wearying when my heart is anchored in the certainty of His return.

THE BLESSED HOPE OF HIS APPEARING

Titus 2:13 calls Christ's return our "blessed hope." It is not a fearful event but a joyful expectation. For the believer, His coming means:

- The end of sorrow.
- The end of suffering.
- The end of death.
- The fullness of eternal life with Him.

When the trumpet sounds, every tear will be wiped away, and the seated saints will rise to reign with their King forever.

PRACTICAL APPLICATIONS

- I must live daily with eternity in view, keeping my eyes on Christ's return.

- I must not be distracted by temporary trials but stay focused on the blessed hope.

- I must keep my lamp burning with faith, prayer, and holiness, ready for His appearing.

- I must use my time wisely, serving faithfully until He comes.

REFLECTION

- Are you living as one who is truly expecting Christ to return?

- How does your hope in His coming shape your decisions and priorities today?

- If He were to come today, would you be found resting in His victory and walking in His authority?

PROPHETIC DECLARATION

I declare that I will live seated in hope until Christ returns. My heart is steadfast, my eyes are lifted, and my spirit is anchored in the blessed hope of His coming. I will endure with joy, walk in authority, and witness with urgency. I will not fear the shaking of this world, for my hope is eternal and my future is secure. Amen.

CLOSING PRAYER

Lord Jesus, thank You for the blessed hope of Your return. Teach me to wait with endurance, live with holiness, and walk with authority until that day. Keep my heart steadfast and my eyes fixed on You. May I never grow weary in waiting but remain faithful in service. Come quickly, Lord Jesus. Until You come, I will live seated in victory and anchored in hope. Amen.

Conclusion

Seated Until the End: The Final Charge

"Sit on my right hand, until I make thine enemies thy footstool." — Hebrews 1:13 (KJV)

THE PICTURE OF VICTORY COMPLETED

From the very first pages of this book, we have journeyed into the heavenly throne room, where Christ reigns, and the earthly battlefield, where His enemies are made His footstool. This divine picture is not only about Christ's exaltation but about the believer's participation in that triumph.

Jesus is seated, not pacing, not striving, not worrying but enthroned in perfect victory. Every enemy is under His feet. And because we are seated with Him (see Ephesians 2:6), His posture becomes our posture. His rest becomes our rest. His victory becomes our victory.

What the Father promised to the Son, that every enemy would become His footstool is also extended to His body, the church. The promise is certain: no enemy, no weapon, no kingdom of darkness will prevail against those who abide in Christ.

ENEMIES UNDER THE FOOTSTOOL

Let us remind ourselves what this means practically. The enemies that once terrified us are now beneath us:

- **Sin** — defeated by the blood of Jesus.
- **Satan** — crushed under the heel of Christ.
- **Fear** — broken by perfect love.
- **Death** — swallowed up in resurrection victory.
- **Opposition** — silenced by divine authority.

What was once over our heads is now under our feet. The Cross turned the tables, and the throne sealed the victory.

THE CALL TO PERSEVERE UNTIL THE END

Although victory is certain, the process of subduing enemies is ongoing. This is why the word is "until." God is progressively working out Christ's triumph on earth until the final day, when every knee bows and every tongue confesses that Jesus Christ is Lord (see Philippians 2:10–11).

For the believer, this means walking in faithful endurance:

- We sit in spiritual rest while God works.

- We stand in spiritual warfare when called to resist.

- We walk in spiritual authority every day until the promise is fulfilled in full.

This is the rhythm of kingdom living: rest, resist, and reign.

A PROPHETIC PICTURE OF THE CHURCH

The church in this hour is called to rise from complacency and reclaim her authority. We are not victims of culture, politics, or demonic activity. We are ambassadors of heaven, kings and priests unto God, carriers of divine power.

The enemy may roar, but his roar is powerless against the decree of the throne. The church must not shrink back in fear but rise up in faith, declaring, **"The Lord is on the throne, and His enemies are under His feet."**

We are a people seated in rest yet standing in boldness. We are a people who walk as overcomers. We are the church victorious.

A CHARGE TO THIS GENERATION

Beloved reader, as you close this book, let these truths be sealed in your heart:

1. **You are Seated** — You don't fight for position; you live from your position in Christ.

2. **You are Secure** — No enemy can dethrone you from where Christ has placed you.

3. **You are Sent** — Authority is not only for your protection but for your mission: to win souls, destroy the works of the devil, and glorify God.

4. **You are Stronger Than You Know** — Not because of who you are in yourself, but because of who you are in Him.

Never again allow the enemy to intimidate you. Rise each morning declaring: **"My life is seated in Christ, my enemies are under my feet, and I will walk in victory until the end."**

FINAL REFLECTION

- Are you living from the place of rest or still striving in your own strength?

- Do you truly believe that every enemy will be subdued under Christ's feet?

- How can you walk more intentionally in daily authority, advancing the kingdom of God?

PROPHETIC DECLARATION

I declare today that I am seated with Christ in heavenly places. The throne is my position, the footstool is my reality, and victory is my inheritance. Every enemy is under my feet. I will walk in triumph, speak with authority, and live with unshakable faith. Until the final day when all things are made subject to Christ, I will endure, I will overcome, and I will glorify God in all things. Amen.

CLOSING PRAYER

Father, thank You for the eternal victory that is found in Christ Jesus. Thank You that I am seated with Him in heavenly places, and that no enemy can overthrow Your decree. Teach me to live from rest, to walk in authority, and to persevere with endurance. May my life reflect the power of the throne and the reality of the footstool. Use me as a vessel of victory in this generation. May I never forget that in Christ, I am more than a conqueror, and that the end has already been secured. To You be glory, honor, and dominion forever. In Jesus' mighty name. Amen.